W9-BOX-951

FRESHWATER ANGELFISHES

KW-048

CONTENTS

Endpapers: Front and back endpapers by H.J. Richter.
Front Cover: CLI
Back Cover: H.J. Richter
Frontis: Klaus Paysan

1995 Edition

Distributed in the UNITED STATES to the Pet Trade by T.F.H. Publications, Inc., One T.F.H. Plaza, Neptune City, NJ 07753; distributed in the UNITED STATES to the Bookstore and Library Trade by National Book Network, Inc. 4720 Boston Way, Lanham MD 20706; in CANADA to the Pet Trade by H & L Pet Supplies Inc., 27 Kingston Crescent, Kitchener, Ontario N2B 2T6; Rolf C. Hagen Ltd., 3225 Sartelon Street, Montreal 382 Quebec; in CANADA to the Book Trade by Vanwell Publishing Ltd., 1 Northrup Crescent, St. Catharines, Ontario L2M 6P5 ; in ENGLAND by T.F.H. Publications, PO Box 15, Waterlooville PO7 6BQ; in AUSTRALIA AND THE SOUTH PACIFIC by T.F.H. (Australia), Pty. Ltd., Box 149, Brookvale 2100 N.S.W., Australia; in NEW ZEALAND by Brooklands Aquarium Ltd. 5 McGiven Drive, New Plymouth, RD1 New Zealand; in Japan by T.F.H. Publications, Japan—Jiro Tsuda, 10-12-3 Ohjidai, Sakura, Chiba 285, Japan; in SOUTH AFRICA by Lopis (Pty) Ltd., P.O. Box 39127, Booysens, 2016, Johannesburg, South Africa. Published by T.F.H. Publications, Inc.

MANUFACTURED IN THE UNITED STATES OF AMERICA
BY T.F.H. PUBLICATIONS, INC.

Freshwater Angelfishes

By Dr. Herbert R. Axelrod
and
Dr. Warren E. Burgess

Two young silver veiltail angelfish. Once breeding techniques were established several varieties such as this one were developed. Photo by Dr. Herbert R. Axelrod. *Below:* A tankful of angelfish is a beautiful sight. Narrow-leaved plant species can be added for esthetic value.

The Beginning

By Dr. Herbert R. Axelrod

It was 1947 and I had just come back from the Army. World War II had been good to me, and instead of going to a real war, I fought the battle of the books . . . the U.S. Army had sent me to college. Now it was 1947 and they promised me another four years of college on the G.I. Bill . . . but I had to stay in the reserve.

I entered New York University and tried to make-do on $90 a month. I had a small apartment in Brooklyn, and my neighbors, Bob and Vivienne Strasbourger, invited me to visit them the first week I was there. We had a natural attraction for one another since we both loved tropical fishes.

Bob was breeding tiger barbs, and he was angry that the small barbs would attack his maturing angelfish, gobbling their fins and tearing them to shreds before they could mature. The angelfish cowered in the corners of the aquarium as the aggressive barbs took over the tank, especially during feeding time. Bob had an extra 20-gallon tank, and he agreed to sell it to me for $5 if I would take care of his angelfish. The deal was made and I quickly set up the tank.

The next weekend Bob brought over the angelfish, and he was very disappointed that my tank was set up with nothing but water! Where were the plants, gravel, heater, etc.? I saw the look on Bob's face and quickly explained that angelfish didn't need all those hiding places if they were kept in a tank by themselves . . . and my apartment was warm enough; besides, the heater used electricity and I had to pay for that. The apartment was steam-heated and the landlord paid for that, so . . . .

The angelfish he gave me, three of them, were about four months old, but their growth had been stunted because they never got a full meal. I quickly put them on a diet of live foods, with freshly collected *Daphnia* always swimming about the tank to serve as a snack and with live tubifex worms which I collected on weekends with Bill Vorderwinkler. In between they were offered scraped, frozen beef heart and dry foods. These were the years before freeze-dried tubifex worms were available . . . and no flake foods either!

The angelfish thrived under this management. Their tank was always between 74 and 80° F., their bellies were always full, and I changed one gallon of water every day. This water changing was done utilizing a one-gallon jug and a siphon tube. I always kept the level of the 20-gallon tank a few inches from the top. I started out by putting a gallon of tap water into a gallon jug I had. I used hot tap water. Within 24 hours of sitting in the sunlight (no cap on the jug) the temperature quickly dropped to the same temperature as the tank or perhaps a bit higher. I then poured the gallon of water into the 20-gallon tank, allowing it to stir up as much debris as possible. I waited for the water to settle down (about 15 minutes) and then siphoned a gallon of water from the bottom of the tank into the jug. I poured the collected water into the toilet bowl, rinsed out the jug with hot water from the tap and set the jug filled with fresh tap water on the window sill again for tomorrow's water change. The system worked wonders, and within eight months I noticed that the angelfish started to gently attack one another.

This attack was not a vicious sort of thing, but rather one fish would make a dart for another one, the attacker would stop short of reaching the fish with its lunge, while the fish being attacked would gracefully move out of the way. This went on for a few days until I noticed that one of the fish was developing a short, thick white tube which projected from near its anal pore. The tank was still bare of any ornaments, so I quickly put into the tank a potted Amazon swordplant which I purchased from the pet shop. While I was at the shop, by the way, I made a deal to sell the angelfish, the price paid depending upon their size. At the size of a 25¢ piece, I would get 25¢ each for them. If they were the size of a 50¢ piece, I would get 50¢ each for them . . . and if they were the size of a silver dollar, that's just what I would get for them! Looking back on the deal, I guess I counted my chickens before they were hatched . . . I was selling fishes which weren't even spawned!

In a few days I noticed that two of the fish hid among the leaves of the Amazon swordplant while the third kept to itself in the open water. The next day I saw that the pair had spawned . . . not on the Amazon swordplant leaf as I had expected, but on the glass in the corner where the black cement made the glass opaque.

This foiled my plans, for I had expected to remove the

A combination of a blacklace angel and a veiltail angel produces a blacklace veiltail as seen here. Even the rays of the ventral fins become elongated. Photo by Dr. Herbert R. Axelrod.

One of the more colorful angelfish is the golden variety shown here. Dark stripes are present in the young but disappear with growth. Photo by H.J. Richter.

eggs and hatch them in a small two-gallon aquarium. Never one to give up, I used the two-gallon aquarium to house the third fish, leaving the pair to hatch their own eggs. Bob came over the next day and noticed a few of the eggs had turned white. Soon more and more eggs turned white until after two days only a dozen of the almost 200 eggs hatched. I didn't have the heart to take the babies away, but the parents took care of the dead, white eggs and carefully managed the wriggling fry which were still attached to the glass. In about five days the babies were free-swimming and I had to begin feeding them.

As soon as the angelfish had laid their eggs I began a hatch of brine shrimp eggs. Unfortunately the eggs didn't produce many newly hatched shrimp, so I had to rely on another first food. I boiled some water and added a chicken egg, allowing the egg to boil for about 15 minutes. I then soaked the egg in ice water to cool it, removed the yolk of the egg and chopped it into small pieces. I then added a bit of water to the egg yolk and finally squeezed it through a cloth (my handkerchief !), allowing the yolk to fall into the tank. I knew the baby angelfish were eating it because their bellies became round . . . and yellow! But I was accumulating a yellow carpet on the tank bottom, too.

I don't know what went wrong, but after a week or so the babies disappeared and I assumed the parents ate them.

I put the third fish back into the tank, and it seemed a lot happier . . . until the pair attacked it. This time the attack was more vicious, with actual contact being made. I could hardly believe my eyes, for I hadn't even noticed that one of the fish had the same white tube protruding from its vent. This tube, the ovipositor, first shows on the female angelfish. A few days later it appears on the male. The female's tube is thicker than the male's, but this difference is difficult to judge for a beginner. The best way to tell which is the male and which the female is, of course, to see which one lays the eggs! Prior to actual spawning you can view the fish from above and the fatter one is probably the female. People who say they can sex angelfish before they are in spawning condition are either bragging, lying or know something I have been unable to prove. Several times I tested so-called experts by asking them to sort out the males and females from ten angelfishes about two inches in size. I allowed them to grow up and nearly always had about as many males among the "females" as I would have expected from a random selection.

For several years I had a fish farm in Florida where we raised 250,000 angelfish a year. I had the help of several professional people. *None* was able to sex angelfish before the female filled with eggs.

MAKING A PROFIT SPAWNING ANGELFISH

Realizing that three is a crowd as far as angelfish are concerned, I decided to isolate the pair and headed for the pet shop with the extra angelfish in an insulated beer can (no plastic bags in those days . . . we used one-gallon beer cans which were insulated with rags, newspaper and "oilcloth"). The pet shop owner was quite a salesman. He had several angelfish about the same size as the one I was trying to sell, so he didn't want to buy mine. Instead, he suggested that I buy three of his and see if they wouldn't pair off. Then I could bring two of them back for a complete refund.

Of course, I had to buy another 20-gallon high aquarium, but I figured it was a wise investment, even though it was my weekly meat money. So home I came with another 20-gallon aquarium, four angelfish and high hopes for beginning an angelfish hatchery.

I took about ten gallons of water from the set up angelfish tank and added it to three gallons of fresh tap water. Making sure the temperature was the same as that in the first angelfish tank, I added the new fish to the bare tank. I also added about five gallons of fresh tap water of the proper

2

(1) A pair of silver angelfish spawning on a broad-leaved plant. (2) Young angelfish starting to take on the shape of their parents. Photo by H.J. Richter. (3) A pair of marble angelfish with strong black markings in the fins.

3

temperature to the old angelfish tank. Maybe it was this fresh water, but the next morning I found a huge spawn on one of the leaves of the Amazon swordplant.

Now came the big decision: should I leave the eggs with the parents or remove them to hatch them artificially? I thought I had better not take a chance, so I decided to remove the leaf and put it into the two-gallon hatching tank. The tank was not set up at all, so I took two gallons of water from the breeding tank. This was the same water in which the eggs were spawned. I added about ten drops of 5% methylene blue to this hatching tank as a fungus preventative. It made the water just blue enough so that you could hardly see through the tank. I then prepared to remove the leaf from the Amazon swordplant.

I was nervous about tearing out the leaf, perhaps shaking off some of the eggs and then exposing the eggs to the air, so I carefully clipped the leaf with scissors as close to the eggs as possible, put the leaf in a water glass (all this was done underwater, of course) and then lifted the glass gently out of the spawning tank. So far, so good! I carefully lowered the glass into the two-gallon tank and set it down in its normal upright position.

As a substitute for the parents, I now had to create a gentle flow of air bubbles over the eggs to simulate the mouthing action of the parents and to ensure a supply of oxygen to the eggs without actually bumping them. Keeping the eggs in a tall glass makes this easy. Usually a small piece of lead "plant anchor" attached to the bottom of the leaf will prevent the leaf from floating out of the glass, especially after you have introduced the air release gadget. I used a small vibrator air pump and attached a long piece of plastic tubing to it. I inserted an inexpensive T-valve in the tubing. The outlet in the T-valve that is controlled was left open, and I connected the air stone in line with the open line. I knew that the back pressure from the air stone would be controlled if I vented the excess air using the control pin in the T-valve.

As I adjusted the stream of bubbles using the T-valve, I looked for the finest bubbles I could manage. Then I lowered the stone into the glass with the leaf and directed the air bubbles away from the eggs. All the water in the glass was affected by the air, and it really didn't matter where I put the air stone as long as the bubbles didn't strike the eggs directly and knock them loose.

The next day I inspected the eggs and found everything had gone wrong. The vibrator pump had slowed down and a mere trickle of air was being released. Nothing I could do to the pump made it produce more air, even when I closed the bleeder valve on the T-valve. Then I took a more drastic step and removed the air stone from the end of the plastic tubing . . . sure enough, that was the problem. When I put the plastic tubing back into the water the massive release of air bubbles indicated that the problem was with the air stone. I tried blowing through the air stone and found that it took a tremendous pressure for the air to pass through. I later found out that the stone became clogged because I had placed the pump on the floor in a very dusty corner. The air picked up by the pump was laden with dust that was pushed into the air stone, which acted as an air filter, clogging itself up.

I put in a new air stone and protected it by placing the pump in a dust-free location. But I went even further. I put the pump in a one-gallon empty paint can after wrapping it in several inches of loose cheesecloth and then surrounded it with aquarium gravel. This not only kept out the dust, but it muffled the unpleasant drone of the vibrator pump as well.

I had expected trouble from this batch of eggs because of the lack of air, and I wasn't disappointed. The second day more and more white eggs showed up, and in a few days more the telltale cotton-like growth of saprolegnid fungus took over and killed even newly-hatched fry. What was in-

1
2
3
4
5
6
7
8

9

10

11

12

13

Scenes from the Rio Negro trip: (1) Smoke pollution on the Amazon. (2) Manaus skyline. (3) and (4) Native houses built on stilts. (5) Native girls. (6) Dr. Axelrod helping Selia Fonte unload. (7) Flooded jungle area. (8) Native with dugout. (9) Native hut in jungle clearing. (10) Houseboat made of same material. (11) Almost impenetrable jungle close by. (12) Native children playing in river. (13) Rio Negro angelfish. Photos by Dr. Herbert R. Axelrod.

teresting in this batch was that a few of the eggs did fall off the leaf. These eggs hatched and the babies eventually grew up.

In a short time the new angelfish spawned and I was quickly buying up odd angelfish from my friends who gave up trying to spawn them. Each 20-gallon tank now had about five pairs of fish, and every week I had at least one spawn. My two-gallon hatching tanks worked fine, each one being outfitted with its own small pump, and the only change in my routine was the substitution of pieces of slate for the Amazon swordplant. (Which was just about out of large leaves!) In the early days (the 1950's through the early 1970's) an all-glass tank was just about unknown. Tanks were made with stainless steel frames and slate bottoms. When tank manufacturers made these slate bottoms they often ended up with strips of slate which had no value in tank-making. The strips were usually about 3 inches wide and 8-10 inches long. These strips, laid at a 60° angle to the aquarium glass, made a fine spawning site for angelfish.

I was soon producing 300 angelfish a week from ten breeding pairs and selling them for 25¢ each after 30 days. The whole trick was to give them a steady diet of newly hatched brine shrimp and sifted *Daphnia*. I fed the fish five times a day in small quantities. A brief description of my brine shrimp hatchery might be of value.

I used five-gallon carboys. These carboys were made of very heavy glass and had a one-inch hole in the top for a cap. I cut the bottom off, turned the carboys upside down and put a stopcock in the one-inch hole, which enabled me to draw water from the bottom of the carboy. I made up my saline (salt) solution using sea salts which I bought from my local pet shop and added enough salt to make the specific gravity about 5% higher than that recommended by the label on the brine shrimp eggs. Different eggs require different salinities.

I put heaters (submergible) in the carboys with aerators. I

used violent aeration from the air stone, which was weighted down and placed at the very bottom in the neck of the carboy. I kept the temperature of the water in the carboys at 85° F. minimum. Sometimes it went to 90° in the summertime. I gave the eggs a few days to hatch and could tell the hatching time as the colors of the churned up water turned from a milk-chocolate brown to a reddish brown. The newly hatched brine shrimp nauplii are red. As soon as the mixture was red enough, I placed a dark cloth over the carboy, turned off the aerator and put a strong light on the bottom of the carboy (outside . . . not in the water!) so the light shone down onto the stopcock. Within an hour the bottom of the carboy was covered with a deep red stain that I recognized as a massive cloud of newly hatched brine shrimp. I then put a quart pot under the stopcock spigot, put a sieve on top and used a very fine-meshed nylon net inside the sieve. I turned on the spigot and the water came into the net laden with newly hatched brine shrimp . . . and no egg shells! I carefully watched the amount of water coming into the pot and turned off the stopcock as it neared the capacity of the pot. I lifted the net, washed the brine shrimp in running cold water for a few seconds and then fed the baby angelfish by scooping some shrimp from the net. The washing merely ensured that I wouldn't get a buildup of salt in the small two-gallon hatching tanks after repeated feedings. I then put the water I had taken from the carboy back into the carboy and added a few more eggs to the total mixture. I could do this for at least ten days, and by having two carboy systems working I found no difficulty in keeping thousands of angelfish fry content.

Eventually my system with ten pairs of working breeders produced 1,000 saleable babies a week . . . and this business grew to the point where I was producing 8,000 month-old angelfish a week (in Florida) and shipping them all over the country. This same type of angelfish hatchery concept flourished in many of the major cities of America,

1
2
3
4
5
6
7
8

9

10

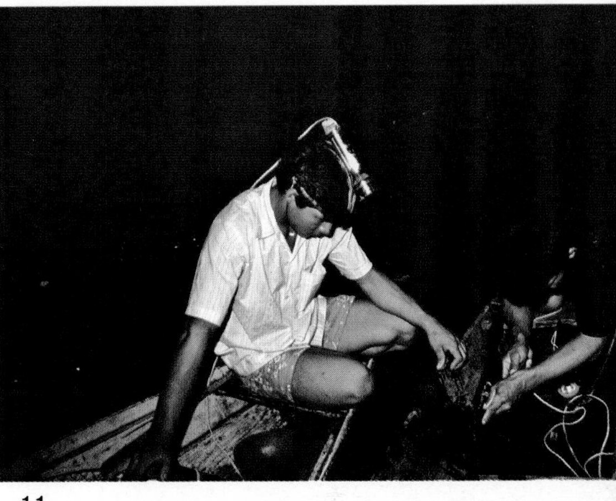

11

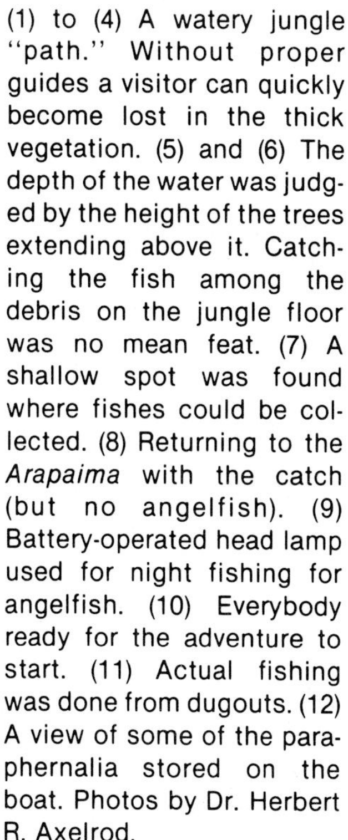

(1) to (4) A watery jungle "path." Without proper guides a visitor can quickly become lost in the thick vegetation. (5) and (6) The depth of the water was judged by the height of the trees extending above it. Catching the fish among the debris on the jungle floor was no mean feat. (7) A shallow spot was found where fishes could be collected. (8) Returning to the *Arapaima* with the catch (but no angelfish). (9) Battery-operated head lamp used for night fishing for angelfish. (10) Everybody ready for the adventure to start. (11) Actual fishing was done from dugouts. (12) A view of some of the paraphernalia stored on the boat. Photos by Dr. Herbert R. Axelrod.

12

and the supply of locally bred angelfish discouraged the establishment of major hatchery centers which could supply the entire country . . . until the fancy varieties came into being.

THE FANCY VARIETIES

In 1952 I saw my first red-spotted angelfish. It was huge . . . perhaps the largest angelfish I had ever seen. I saw it in a wholesaler's establishment in Brooklyn. The man's name was Henry Hessel . . . but I don't remember the name of his business. Henry Hessel had nine of these "new" angelfish, and I bought all of them. He had imported three German cans filled with six angelfish each, so there were nine fish which Henry had sold to another breeder of angelfish. Later on I discovered these fish were from British Guiana (now known as Guyana) and they were the typical wild angelfish . . . they looked so different from the colorless, inbred angelfish I was producing.

I tried in many, many ways . . . changing foods, pH, DH, light . . . but I never was able to produce eggs. As a matter of fact, I even bought this same kind of fish from other importers, but to no avail. As far as I can ascertain no one ever spawned these wild fish from Guyana, nor did they ever spawn any angelfish from the wilds of northern South America. It was only the Amazonian angelfish which eventually was spawned, and the offspring from this population became the basis for all the angelfish spawned in the world.

Subsequently I became so "psyched" over my inability to spawn these spotted angelfish that I decided to go to British Guiana and collect my own. I had heard that many of the fishes shipped from there were drugged so they couldn't spawn. The gold tetra, *Hemigrammus armstrongi*, seemed to be another fish from British Guiana which couldn't be duplicated. (We later discovered that the "gold" was a disease which was not passed on to the offspring . . . so the gold tetras became silver tetras after the first generation!)

Flying into Georgetown, British Guiana was pleasant, and I could hardly wait to get into the jungle and collect angelfish. It took only a few days for me to get into the bush and start fishing. In a week I had collected every fish that was ever shipped out of British Guiana . . . except the angelfish. I finally got some help from an Asian Indian gentleman. He took me to a "secret" stream, and after a few hours of fishing I caught three adult, mature angelfish. Later on he told me they fished for angelfish at night using a strong flashlight and a long-handled net. But I had the fish I wanted and I was only too pleased to leave the hot, mosquito-laden area for the comfort of an air-conditioned room in Georgetown. Subsequently I was unable to spawn these fish either.

When in doubt, read. I did just this. After studying everything available about angelfishes, I discovered they are found all over the northern part of South America and I began a systematic collection of these different species. Dr. Warren Burgess, my associate and co-author of this book, will treat the differences between the species in his review, but when I started looking for angelfishes, I had five species to look for . . . what a disappointment to discover that most of them were all the same species.

It really doesn't matter. I brought back hundreds of angelfishes from every population in South America, including those found in the Amazon, in the Rio Negro north of the Amazon, south of the Amazon near Humaita, in Peru . . . but neither I nor anyone I met was ever able to spawn any of them. This holds true for not only the professional breeders, but such world-famous experts as Dr. Eduard Schmidt-Focke, Hans Joachim Richter and perhaps the largest importer of wild angelfishes, Mr. Heiko Bleher.

In the late 1950's Southeast Asia, especially Hong Kong and Singapore, were quickly becoming tropical aquarium fish breeding centers. They began breeding angelfish by

1

2

Scenes from the Humaita trip: (1) The Tranzamazonica Highway (unpaved of course) leading off into the jungle towards Humaita. (2) Two interesting *Corydoras* species were collected in this small stream. Photos by Dr. Herbert R. Axelrod. (3) This pool, only 50 yards across, produced thousands of *Dianema* and *Pterophyllum*. (4) Dr. Gery, Adolf, and a native assistant working a finger of one of the larger pools. Photos by Dr. Herbert R. Axelrod.

3

4

the millions, carefully tending their fish with intensive care, almost hand-feeding each fish. With this tender loving care it wasn't long before they discovered "sports" or "mutants" with longer fins than the normal. These long-finned mutants couldn't swim as well as their normal brethren and they usually died because they could not compete for food. The Chinese breeders of Southeast Asia, always eager to produce new varieties (remember what they did for goldfish), sought fish with new shapes and new colors. They would isolate these freaks hoping to raise them to breeding size. In a few years they had produced angelfish with long fins. These fish were called "veiltails," the same term applied to the long-finned goldfish.

At about the same time a breeder in Holland was able to produce a half-black angelfish. This was an angelfish normal in all respects except that the rear half of its body was black, while the front half was normally pigmented. This strain would have been very popular had the almost completely black angelfish not shown up in Singapore. Though initially the black angelfish was hardly as black as a black molly, constant inbreeding did produce a strain of black angelfish . . . and these were then crossed with the veiltails, producing black veiltail angelfish.

Soon other varieties made their appearance. A fish with almost no skin pigmentation appeared. This variety showed its vital organs through its skin and earned the strain the name "bleeding heart angelfish." Another strain was produced which had no black stripes, and this fish became the "ghost angelfish."

Perhaps the most elusive of all color varieties was the albino. As with all domesticated species of animals, albinos usually turn up rather frequently. But the albino angelfish, even though it appeared from time to time, was never fertile and no one was ever able to induce an albino to spawn, even though they tried to cross it with a normal angelfish.

One of the wierdest examples of an angelfish color variety

was produced by an angelfish breeder in Singapore from ghost angelfish I had sent him years before (the complete story follows).

This angelfish started out looking for all the world like a normal angelfish. The only thing different about it was that the parents were ghosts and almost colorless, but the offspring were normal. I brought a few of these baby fish to Hans Joachim Richter in Leipzig, East Germany so he could photograph their transition. AS THE FISH GREW IN SIZE THEIR COLORS WOULD CHANGE. This is not an unknown phenomenon in the world of fishes, but for angelfishes it was something else.

All the angelfish which we knew before had the same coloration as their parents. But here we had some almost colorless ghost angelfish throwing off normally colored fry that changed colors as they grew up. They reach about breeding size when the black starts to fade. Instead of the complete pigmentation disappearing as it did in their parents, only the melanophores or black pigments are broken down, and the red and yellow pigments stay. This produces fish which are mostly red, yellow and gold. In some specimens the black pigment in the eye also disappears, thus producing an "albino." Unfortunately this genetic effect doesn't appear until the fish are mature, for inbreeding these fish produces normally colored offspring . . . offspring, by the way, which never lose their colors!! It seems that only the offspring from that particular pair of fish went through this metamorphosis . . . and how lucky I was that I brought some to Richter so he could photograph all the color phases through which these angelfish passed.

Finding new color or finnage varieties is up to you, the amateur breeder. Pay particular attention to your fish as soon as the eggs hatch. Look for one that looks or acts differently than the others. Isolate this individual and see what it grows up to be. That's the best way to find new varieties.

In a pinch the flashlight can be held in one's mouth so that the hands remain free. *Below:* One of the stopping-off places near Manaus where the Amazon and Rio Negro Rivers meet. Photos by Dr. Herbert R. Axelrod.

The Heavenly Paradox

By Dr. Herbert R. Axelrod

The greatest of all dreams are those that can never be fulfilled. Some men dream about flying like a bird . . . or diving into the sea 1,000 meters in free-dive (and coming back to tell about it) . . . my dream has been to photograph every fish in the world. Since a dream can be fulfilled a little at a time, I decided to photograph my fishes genus by genus, and I started with the two genera closest to my heart (and having the fewest species) . . . *Symphysodon,* the discusfishes, and *Pterophyllum,* the angelfishes. I had already photographed and collected every known species of discus, and now I was about to set out to collect the missing link in the angelfishes.

When Dr. Leonard P. Schultz worked up the genus *Pterophyllum* he included in his writeup a map showing the distribution of the various species. His map showed no collections of angelfish in the Rio Negro of Brazil, from Manaus through Barcelos. This area is famous for its unique fauna, since it contains the beautiful cardinal tetra, *Cheirodon axelrodi*, and the blue discus, *Symphysodon discus.* The blue discus is an example of the area's unique fauna, since it is found only in the Rio Negro, but the cardinal tetra has been found as far away as Colombia.

In September of 1975 I planned a trip up the Rio Negro to collect all three fishes . . . the cardinal tetra, the blue discus and the missing angelfish. As usual my trip started in Manaus, where Willi Schwartz (Aquario Rio Negro, P.O. Box 381, Manaus, Amazonas, Brazil) has his fleet of boats used solely for collecting aquarium fishes. Willi loaned me a boat and full crew. I was lucky that the crew was composed mainly of Indians from the region of the black water (Rio Negro). My crew chief was Selia Alfonso Fonte; he had his wife, Rainumda, with us as cook; the engineer was Christian de Braga; and the fisherman was Manoel Nena, who brought his five-year-old son along as our helper. Raul Fonte, father of Selia, also accompanied us because he knew several Indian dialects.

As we left Manaus at high noon on the 7th of September, I was amazed at the modern-looking skyline of the city. Since it became a free port, Manaus has been growing and growing, until now it is a modern city with traffic jams, water shortages and brown-outs. It was delightful to get farther out of town and lose sight of the huge white concrete superstructures, and the air started to smell sweet . . . then I saw it! Ugly black smoke pouring out of a chimney, defacing the beautiful blue sky with a horrible scar. The jungle was being robbed of its wood and life-giving oxygen capability to make a very cheap quality plywood. Already filth and debris were being dumped into the Rio Negro.

How long would it take to make the magnificent Rio Negro another Hudson or Danube or Thames, where slime and filth kill every edible fish? I was even happy to pass the houses of some of the workers where the Oriental technique of waste disposal was utilized . . . with the outhouse standing on posts over the water, feeding the fish human waste. But this sophistication degenerated into areas farther up the Rio Negro where the whole house was elevated above the water! The advantage of this sort of building was that it kept out most of the crawling things, including (but not limited to) snakes, scorpions, rats, cats, dogs, beetles, spiders and kids. It also kept the house pretty clean . . . no messy basements to worry about!

It only took us three days in our Deutz 3-cylinder powered diesel boat, 45 feet long, to make it to Igarape Anapichi and Igarape Apania. These are two large ditches which swell to 1000 yards in width during the high water season; they always contain blue discus hiding at the bases of the submerged trees and logs. I could hardly wait for us to find a sandy beach on which to land. I pulled out the gangplank, walked down the skin-polished board and had Selia hand me the nets. We picked this particular landing spot because there were a few Indian houses there and it had a sandy beach as contrasted to a flooded area where there is no beach at all. In a few minutes two beautiful girls came out to greet me. Their home was a thatched roof hut raised about 5 feet off the ground to protect it from rising waters.

This was exceptionally high water for September, and some people said the water was 30 feet higher than normal. I could believe it, for when we took two dugouts into the "jungle" to look around we found the jungle was UNDERNEATH us and the only things sticking out of the water were trees over 40 feet high!!

We kept going into the jungle, deeper and deeper until we arrived at trees which grew higher. This meant, of course, that the water was lower, since the only way we could judge the depth of the water was by the height of the trees. Naturally those trees growing on hills looked taller, since they stuck out of the water more. Finally we were joined by other Indians, who took us to an area where we could stand in knee-deep water. I gently stepped into the coffee-black water; I couldn't see where I was stepping, since the bottom was invisible. I looked like the "great white hunter" with my plaid shirt and straw hat, quite in contrast to some of the Indians. There were thousands of tiny fishes moving about, and catching them with so much debris in the water would be quite a problem. The bottom was soft and gentle because it had several feet of leaves padding each of my steps. These leaves were brewing like tea leaves, gently turning the water blacker and blacker as the rain tried in vain to dilute the tannic acid. The pH was rather high (for the Rio Negro) at this time, almost 5.0, and the water temperature varied from 82 degrees to 90 degrees, with an air temperature of 84 degrees. How proud I was of the accurate thermometer that I used! Dr. Schultz had given it to me in 1953!

We cleared an area about 20 feet square and collected some of the fishes. They were mostly tetras of a rather unspectacular color, but a beautiful striped *Leporinus,* a lovely dwarf cichlid and a score of 2-inch-long piranhas were the highlights of our efforts. Where were the discus and angelfish? Didn't you know these fish hide and run away from the slightest disturbances during the day? You might catch the occasional angelfish with a seine, but try catching a discus! Never!

So, back to the boat "Arapaima." By the way, the name "Arapaima" is the name of the largest Amazonian fish, *Arapaima gigas.* This boat was named after the fish because when it was named it was the largest boat that Willi had . . . today it is the smallest! The fish business was good to Willi, I guess.

On the boat we had a little siesta. I had my usual meal . . . spaghetti. I ate spaghetti, by the way, every day for 10 days; it was the only food I had. We couldn't catch fish large enough to eat since the water was so high, and our 50-foot seines were useless . . . so all we had was spaghetti and sun-dried, smelly beef. I preferred the spaghetti.

At 7 p.m. it was time to get up. Night-fishing for angelfish and discus was on the schedule, and I was so excited I could hardly wait. I jumped into the dugout with my waterproof flashlight, two dipnets and a plastic box and was ready to go. I felt a little foolish as I waited almost an hour for the rest of the crew to come with me. Selia and his wife showed me their secret weapon. They took an ordinary flashlight and attached it to a headpiece which was quite comfortable. Then, using a regular automobile battery, they had hours of power . . . and a strong rechargeable battery. My dry cells lasted only an hour! The team of the husband and wife Fonte was remarkable. They spoke very few words, but Mrs. Fonte would light a cigarette and shove it into her husband's mouth, whether he wanted it or not. Finally everything was ready, and we quietly paddled the few hundred yards from our parked boat to the thick trees. I fished in the same boat as Selia Fonte; two other boats joined us, fishing in other areas.

We were very quiet and heard every little noise. Expertly, Selia pulled the boat through the trees, slowly and methodically training his head-mounted flashlight into the water. Though the water was black, the light could penetrate about a foot deep, and the shiny, reflective quality of the scales of a fish was so obvious that we didn't miss very much. Suddenly I saw a telltale shine. It took me a few seconds to recognize that it was an angelfish, but I carefully netted the fish, slowly bringing the net up under it. The fish was about six inches under the surface of the water and resting almost against a tree, protected from almost all sides and from below. We caught about eight angelfish that

1
2
3

night, and here are the notes from my diary: "The two specimens of *Pterophyllum* which were under 5 cm. were long-finned and dark. Certainly this is the stock from which the long-finned and black angels derived. They were not hybrids after all!! Maybe that's why no one ever stepped forward to take credit for having developed them??" By the time I was able to photograph them, they had faded substantially, but they still showed a lot of black on their bodies and in their fins. As I studied the angelfish I became more and more excited!! Their dorsal fins were twice as long as their anal fins. This gave them a very weird appearance . . . like the marine Moorish idol! Possibly this was a new species. The more I studied them, the more I was sure they were something important. I could hardly wait to get back to compare them with *Pterophyllum altum,* which I found even higher up the Rio Negro. But I still had lots of fishing days ahead, for even after having found enough of the missing links in the distribution of the angelfish in the Amazon River system, I still had discus and cardinals to collect . . . and to write about, since no one has ever photographed their range and habitat. I'll let Warren Burgess finish the story about my new angelfishes!

(1) During the time of the high water, most transportation is accomplished by means of simple dugouts. (2) In this area a beautiful species of *Leporinus,* a lovely dwarf cichlid and some small piranhas were captured. (3) Moving along the Rio Negro after a successful collecting trip, one is filled with a mixture of happy satisfaction and sadness, the sadness due to the imminent departure from this beautiful area. Photos by Dr. Herbert R. Axelrod.

One of the signs pointing the way to the eventual destination. Note that the road here is paved. *Below:* with the net set in place to cut off a portion of this pool, few fishes could escape the concerted efforts of the collecting team. Photos by Dr. Herbert R. Axelrod.

A Dream Come True . . . Finding The Southernmost Angelfish

By Dr. Herbert R. Axelrod

Our first night out of Manaus, Brazil was fun! Adolf Schwartz and I slept in sleeping bags (it gets cold at night in the jungle), Heiko Bleher slept in the car and Jacques Gery and Guy van den Bossche slept on foam rubber mattresses. Just as we were falling asleep the rainy season started! Up we jumped, howling with laughter as we tried in vain to protect our clothes and sleeping gear from getting soaked! More danger appeared as we pulled away from our campsite. The friendly, dusty highway was now a slick, slimy, slippery ribbon—the previously obvious potholes were now filled with muddy water which made them impossible to

see even with the headlight beams from the truck. One slip and we would be off the highway with no one to help us, if indeed help would do any good. We slowly plodded along toward Humaita, a few miles an hour, with our previous enthusiasm considerably dampened.

I can't tell you how surprised I was on our second day past Manaus to find a pool filled with thousands of *Dianema urostriata, Dianema longibarbis* and *Pterophyllum scalare.* (During the dry season when winds and sun scorch the jungle and evaporate the water, the small streams and ditches dry up, but not the deep pools found at the end of the corrugated tunnels. These are always filled with fishes and, depending upon when you get there, you might find only a few species of large predatory fishes such as piranhas or you might be lucky, as we were, to find thousands of small catfishes and angelfish.) This pool didn't have a living plant in it, no place for the fishes to hide and nothing for them to feed on, yet they were all healthy and all the same size. The angelfish were about half-grown and about three months of age. I have NEVER found the angelfish of Brazil in schools, yet there were untold thousands in this pool and, much to Adolf Schwartz's delight, they were reachable by car on a long day's drive. This pool, by the way, was just outside of Humaita on the far side of the river; that is, the side you have to reach by ferryboat. Now our enthusiasm was renewed and, once having found this treasure, we decided to make Humaita our headquarters, but not before we could satisfy Heiko's basic reason for the trip.

A few years ago I discovered in Venezuela a magnificent black cichlid that was eventually named *Chuco axelrodi* by Dr. Fernandez-Yepez (it is now more properly called *Cichlasoma axelrodi*). On his previous trip Heiko had found this very same fish in Brazil along the highway that runs east from Humaita, and he promised to try to bring some back alive. We agreed to go along with Heiko to find the new black cichlid, as I wanted some for my own aquarium, too. So off we went from Humaita, a small VW and a VW Kombi raising a cloud of red dust that was visible for miles. (You would think that the floor of the jungle would be fabulous topsoil, but it isn't. Perhaps there are three to eight inches of good black topsoil at the base of the jungle, but underneath that topsoil is nothing but red sand which, once it dries, becomes a fine red powder. As soon as the protective layer of the jungle mat is removed, as it was when the road was built, the rain washes away the topsoil and exposes the red sand.) In order not to breathe too much dust, we arranged that Heiko would drive the small car ten minutes ahead of our truck, since there was almost no other traffic on the road and it took about that long for the dust to subside.

Along the road from Manaus to Humaita we were able to buy gasoline every few hundred kilometers, but on the main Transamazonica Highway running from Humaita through the interior we didn't have such luck. The first three gas stations we stopped at told us they had no gas, so without reaching our goal, which was the river where the black cichlid lived, we turned back. Unfortunately, Heiko didn't know we had turned back! Our signals were crossed and the poor guy spent two days without food or water driving around looking for us!

While we were waiting for Heiko at the Humaita ferry crossing of the Rio Madeira, we fished in several creeks and lakes and found some interesting fishes—though nothing as startling as a cardinal tetra. The highlight of the fishing may have been our trip into the area near Lake Paradise (Lago Paraiso). This lake could be reached only by walking through the jungle for about an hour. We left Dr. Gery to guard the truck while we climbed over fallen trees, and we found the lake with the help of a fisherman. Once at the lake the fisherman took us out in a small canoe and we looked for fish. How lucky we were to see another fisherman using a cast net in the middle of the lake. We immediately made our way over to him and searched through his catch for something interesting. I saw my first example of a large, elongated piranha. NEW! "No," said Dr. Gery later, "that's *Serrasalmus elongatus.*" I was constantly amazed at Gery's ability to identify fishes he had known only from bleached-out museum specimens. What a genius he is! Our fisherman told us that the name of this lake was "Lago Las Pupunhas," but I have no way of knowing whether the spelling is correct, since the lake isn't on any map. We also found one specimen of a small adult angelfish.

When we got back to the road Heiko still had not shown up, so we decided to go back to Humaita. Perhaps Heiko had passed us during the night while we slept at a local hotel. These local hotels are interesting. The room we slept in was occupied the night before by a milk cow! Milk cows are very valuable in Brazil. They do help keep the flies and mosquitoes happy, though, and in addition, our *Off* insect repellent worked very well. At the hotel we entertained ourselves shooting pool. All along the Transamazonica Highway, and along every Brazilian highway in the jungle, we found pool tables. For about 15¢ a game we became experts!

Once we were back in Humaita we began asking the local people about fish. Yes, they knew about the black cichlid, but when we got to where it was supposed to be, it turned out to be merely a dark variety of *Cichlasoma severum.* After lots of wild goosechases, Heiko finally showed up, told me what an "amigo da onca" I was and rushed off driving straight back to Manaus! We didn't feel too ambitious after that, so we decided to hang around Humaita and fish.

That afternoon we headed west along the road from Humaita to Labrea. We made it as far as Rio Ipixuna when an army guard stopped us and told us we could go no further because the road was out. Later we found out that the Indians were giving the army some trouble and more soldiers had been brought in to quell the problem—poor Indians! So we fished in streams along the way back to Humaita.

The Rio Ipixuna is really a part of the Rio Purus, and we expected to find completely different fishes from those found near Humaita, which is on the Rio Madeira. In our first little stream we found nothing, but in other streams we finally saw some interesting catfishes. Trying to catch them was another story, though. So I put a net on both ends of a segment of the stream and used a chemical to bring them to the top so we could see what was so beautiful. We got lots of nice fishes and a few really beautiful giant *Corydoras* species. I thought they were new and we moved on, quite excited about them, when we were approached by the guard who had earlier refused to allow us across the Rio Ipixuna ferry. He wanted some batteries so he could use his radio. I said I would give him the batteries only if he allowed us to fish on the other side of the river for the "acara preto" (the black cichlid) and "acara discu" (discusfish). He said he could not allow us to fish there but if we gave him batteries he would catch some for us that night. I agreed. When we returned to the site that night the guard had one harpooned discus and lots of large *Cichla ocellaris* which he offered us as food! Even though he had no black cichlids I gave him the batteries.

That night, on the way back to Humaita, we again passed the place where we had put chemicals in the stream. I suggested we stop there; Guy and Adolf agreed, so I took out the flashlight and showed Guy and Adolf how to catch fish at night. The fish are actually blinded and stunned by the light, so you merely hold the net in front of them, touch their tail with your toe and into the net they swim! The boys had lots of fun catching fish with me that night, and after that they became ardent night fishermen. The previously treated spot was now loaded with fish, and the size of the *Corydoras* was amazing! They were almost four inches long, and we had two new species of *Corydoras* in one net. Ah, one of these must be named in honor of Heiko Bleher, so later, when I sent the specimens to Dr. Nijssen in Holland, I asked him to name one of the fish *Corydoras bleheri* when the description was published, which he agreed to do.

All told, our trip netted 15 new species in just two weeks! "Not bad," I told Heiko. "But you didn't get the black cichlid, and that's what we came here for!"

It's 10 p.m., Friday night, November 12th, 1976, as I am writing this article. On Sunday, November 14th, I am again leaving for Brazil to look for the black cichlid, *Chuco axelrodi.* Someone offered $500.00 for a pair of them delivered alive and well. If I don't get them this time, I'll double the reward and make it a $1,000 offer to anyone who brings a live pair to my office in Neptune, New Jersey! But they have to be the first pair brought back alive!

Coming back from Humaita we were loaded with fish, exposed films and much anxiety to show Willi Schwartz that we found new *Corydoras*—and at a time when *Corydoras* were out of season in the rest of Brazil and were bringing their highest prices! All Adolf could think of was that he could sell every *Dianema urostriata* for $1.00 each—and there were thousands upon thousands of them in one flood pool!

We drove hard, slowing down temporarily for the sudden, short squalls that heralded the oncoming rainy season. The road was very treacherous when it was wet, as we were constantly reminded when we saw the skeletons of rusted-out cars lying at the bottom of ravines along the road. Since it is not too comfortable driving in the heat, three in the front and one in a sealed rear compartment of the truck without a direct air supply, bouncing along a dirt road, we finally decided, after ten hours of driving, to stop for a little sleep. The night was crisp and beautiful and the sky was filled with as many stars as there were trees in the jungle. It was glorious . . . until we were attacked by more mosquitoes than I had ever seen in my long jungle life! Using nets, repellent and sleeping bags, wearing heavy clothes and remaining inside the truck were to no avail, for even if we could insulate ourselves against the menacing bites of these nasty creatures, we could not sleep because of the wailing drone of their hordes! Can you imagine what millions of mosquitoes sound like when you are trying to sleep? We couldn't sleep, so we went on, finally arriving at the last ferry at midnight.

Would you believe that the last ferry doesn't operate at night? That's right, there was a long line of cars and trucks waiting for the ferry—nothing to do but wait until the mosquitoes arrived! The same millions let us have it again! Even the Indians were being driven crazy, as their spastic-like responses to each bite emphasized. How could we get out of this hell-hole?

Ah! An idea! Let's use a bit of Yankee ingenuity! I spoke to several other people and we chipped in and hired a motor launch (the one that usually pulls the ferry barge across the Amazon) to take us over as passengers without our truck. Two hours later we were in the hotel in Manaus. Adolf returned the next morning, picked up the truck and brought it back. Fortunately for Heiko, he made it back the day before the rains brought the hatching of millions of mosquitoes!

The new *Corydoras* we collected were so unusual that we decided to try to bring them back alive. This meant constantly changing the water in order to keep them from becoming overheated. The task posed no serious problems and we were able to bring them all back without a single casualty. Adolf took the *Corydoras* back to show his father, and I took some dwarf cichlids, a pair of angelfish and six feet of something the Indians smoke! The fish are swimming in my New Jersey water right at this moment. Dr. Burgess verified they were *Pterophyllum scalare.*

1 2

3

4

(1) Almost every bit of water that could possibly support fish life was examined. This even included the small pool at the bottom of the photo. (2) Left to right: Dr. Jaques Gery, Adolf Schwartz and Dr. Herbert R. Axelrod. (3) Who would even guess that this pool would contain thousands of fishes? (4) This pool was formed by the erosive action of water flowing through this corregated drain. Guy van den Bossche is already fishing.

Pterophyllum scalare altum from the Orinoco. Photo by Dr. Herbert R. Axelrod. *Below:* A pair of young aquarium raised *Pterophyllum scalare scalare.* Photo by Dr. Herbert R. Axelrod.

The Species of Angelfishes (Pterophyllum)

By Dr. Warren E. Burgess

One would think that the common aquarium fishes should have no problems concerning their proper scientific names, especially if they have been in the hobby for many years. But in many of the popular aquarium fishes a name is generally applied, usually by a scientist, which is immediately accepted by all concerned, and no further inquiry is made. And after all, since they are common, specimens should be readily available for investigation by scientists in case some question arises as to their proper identity. Unfortunately this is not always the case. Local breeders are often successful in propagating the initially high-priced imports,

and domestic stocks soon are plentiful enough at low prices to satisfy most of the needs of aquarists. The imports naturally drop off considerably as domestic supplies increase and eventually stop altogether. In addition, easy-to-breed species that are genetically variable are selectively bred to produce any number of strains often quite different in appearance from the natural species. Wild-caught specimens are therefore not as available through the aquarium trade as one would think. Any inquiries into the systematic problems of such fishes would necessitate visits to museums where collections of the species concerned are held or travel to their natural habitats (as was done by Dr. Herbert R. Axelrod). The common angelfishes of the genus *Pterophyllum* seem to be one of these groups that has caused a great deal of trouble.

The first angelfish ever described was a species called *Zeus scalaris* by Lichtenstein in 1823. It was collected in "Brazil" and apparently deposited in the Berlin Museum. Cuvier (or Valenciennes) found the specimen there labeled *Zeus scalaris* and was probably unaware that Lichtenstein had already published its description. They therefore described it as new, kept the specific name *scalaris*, but decided that it was in the wrong genus, naming it *Platax ? scalaris.* They apparently were not satisfied with placing it in the genus *Platax* (hence the question mark) and thought that when it became better known (the specimen was in a "mutilated" condition and only an incomplete description could be given) a new genus could be erected for it. This was apparently accomplished some nine years later (in 1840) by Heckel, who was able to see additional specimens from the Rio Negro. He called the new genus *Pterophyllum* (meaning *fins like leaves*), which included at that time the single species *Pterophyllum scalaris.* In 1855 Castelnau described a new genus and species of this same type fish, calling it *Plataxoides dumerilii,* seemingly unaware of the fish described by Cuvier and Valenciennes. Guenther, in his *Catalogue of the Fishes in the British Museum (Natural History),* simplified everything by synonymizing *Plataxoides* with *Pterophyllum* and placing all the species thus far described (*Platax scalaris, Pterophyllum scalaris,* and *Plataxoides dumerilii,* but not *Zeus scalaris* of which he was probably unaware) under the slightly modified name *Pterophyllum scalare.* There were then either one (*P. scalare*) or two (*P. scalare* and *P. dumerilii*) species of angelfishes depending upon whether one agreed with Guenther or not. At least they were finally placed together in a single genus. In 1903 another angelfish species, *Pterophyllum altum,* was described by Pellegrin, and in 1928 a fourth species, *P. eimekei* Ahl, was added to the list. The most recent species described, *Plataxoides leopoldi* Gosse, was placed in Castelnau's genus because Gosse believed that the name *Pterophyllum* was preoccupied by a genus of insects called *Pterophyllum* Harris. But Schultz, in reviewing the genus *Pterophyllum* in 1967, checked on the name and found that Harris consistently used the name *Pterophylla,* not *Pterophyllum* as erroneously reported. The genus name *Pterophyllum* was therefore free to be used (or *available* according to the terminology of the International Rules of Nomenclature).

At this point in time there were five named or nominal species: *Pterophyllum scalare, P. dumerilii, P. altum, P. eimekei* and *P. leopoldi.* But how many *real* species of angelfishes were there?

It seems that Schultz was able to examine the holotype of *P. dumerilii* and the paratypes of *P. leopoldi* and concluded that they are one and the same species. Comparisons of *P. scalare* specimens with those of *P. eimekei* led Schultz to consider the latter species a synonym of the former. The remaining species, *P. altum,* he considered valid although casting some doubt on this decision with his statement, *"Undoubtedly* P. altum *represents the* P. scalare *type of angelfish in the upper Orinoco, and in having a higher average number of dorsal, anal, oblique scale rows, and vertebrae than* P. scalare, *it might be considered to represent only a subspecies of* P. scalare; *however, since* P. altum *has been taken so far only in the upper Orinoco basin, I prefer tentatively to recognize it as a distinct species."*

In recent collections by Dr. Herbert R. Axelrod in the Rio Negro (see "The Heavenly Paradox"), some very interesting and, as it turns out, very important specimens of angelfishes were taken.* According to Schultz' distributional map, the collecting sites for which he had data on the angelfishes were restricted to the Amazon River from its mouth to Manaus and then along the Solimoes (Amazonas) branch of the river to Peru. There were no collections reported on by him from the Rio Negro, which winds its way northwestward toward the Orinoco where *Pterophyllum altum* comes from! These specimens from the Rio Negro thus filled a very important gap. The question as to whether they would show (1) a close association with the Amazon and Solimoes forms and be as different from *P. altum* as they were, (2) a close association with the Orinoco forms and be different from the Amazon and associated forms, or (3) would they show a continuous gradient or cline from Manaus to the Orinoco, indicating that *P. altum* was really not very different after all, could at last be answered. According to Schultz, the differences between *P. altum* and *P. scalare* are the greater average number of soft dorsal and anal fin rays as well as the greater average number of oblique scale rows and vertebrae of *P. altum.*

---

*Because of Dr. Axelrod's report on the short anal fin, I examined the rays carefully under a microscope. It seems fairly certain that the trailing anal rays and sometimes the caudal and pelvic rays were torn or bitten off and have started to regenerate. When I explained this to Dr. Axelrod he surmised that the exceptionally high waters conjugated the habitats of the angelfish with those of the piranhas, thus enabling the piranhas to bite off their long trailing anal fins. Normally the two habitats are distinct and these physical anomalies are not apparent.

The color patterns were said to be identical and therefore of no use in distinguishing the two. Proportional measurements were made but considered unreliable due to the great variability "even at nearly equal sizes," although photos of *P. altum* always seemed to show a fish with more elongate dorsal and anal fins.

When the average number of dorsal and anal fin rays and oblique scale rows were plotted on a map of the Amazon system, it was found that Belem specimens had an average of 24.9 dorsal fin rays, 27.5 anal fin rays and 36.7 oblique scale rows. The average numbers dropped as one headed up-river to Porto do Moz and Santarem (to 23.3 and 22.6 dorsal fin rays, 25.3 and 24.9 anal fin rays and 33.2 and 33.1 oblique scale rows respectively) but increased again (to 24.6, 26.8, and 35.4) by the time one reached Manaus. At this point the branching off of the Rio Negro occurs. If one follows the Solimoes (Amazonas) the counts stay about the same at least as far as Tefe (24.6, 27.1, and 35.5) but start to drop again upstream at Tonantins (23.6, 24.9, and 33.1). With the new specimens available it was discovered that if one follows the Rio Negro from Manaus, the counts increase with distance from the Amazon so that at Igarape Anapichi and Igarape Apania in the upper Rio Negro the average soft dorsal ray count for nine individuals was 26.2, the average anal fin soft ray count 28.3 and the average number of oblique scale rows 38.1. The identification of these specimens as either *P. scalare* or *P. altum* on the basis of counts was not immediately obvious, although they seemed to favor the latter species. Another group of six specimens collected further up the Rio Negro fell nicely into this sequence, with an average number of soft dorsal fin rays of 28.0, anal fin rays 29.8 and oblique scale rows 40.3.* When compared to the counts for *P. altum* from the

---

*The counts that appeared in position 2 on the map appearing in *T.F.H. Magazine* for January 1976, p. 95, were in error.

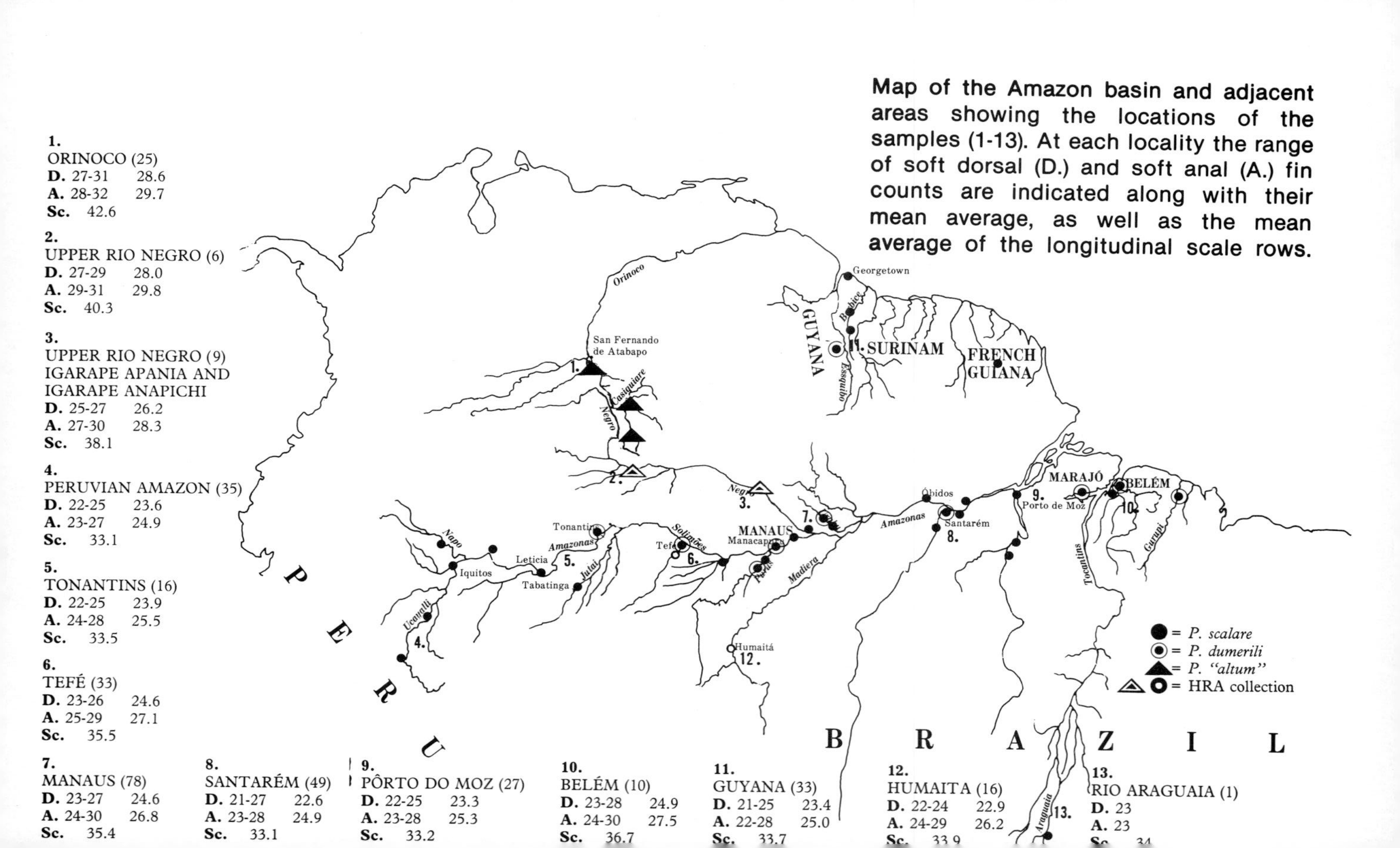

Map of the Amazon basin and adjacent areas showing the locations of the samples (1-13). At each locality the range of soft dorsal (D.) and soft anal (A.) fin counts are indicated along with their mean average, as well as the mean average of the longitudinal scale rows.

Orinoco (28.6, 29.7 and 42.6 respectively) it could be seen that they were extremely close. The Rio Negro angelfishes appear to bridge the gap between the Orinoco populations and the Amazon populations, although still favoring the former.

When one looks at the color pattern of these fish very little can be seen to separate them at first glance. On closer examination, however, certain distinctions become evident. If one were again to compare the extremes (Rio Orinoco with the Amazon or Guyana specimens) one would observe that the Amazon and Guyana specimens possess a dark band that extends from the chest (where it is joined by the corresponding opposite band) through the eye to the first spines of the dorsal fin. The Orinoco forms have a similar band that starts from the same spot on the chest, passes through the eye and ends on the nape. A second band starts from the first few spines of the dorsal fin and extends toward the pectoral fin base but is considerably faded, almost absent, below the first few millimeters. There is a distinct gap between these two bands. The question then arises, how are these bands arranged in the Rio Negro angelfish? It appears that they are similar in position to those of the Orinoco angelfish. The difference in these two types of banding is not all that great. All it takes to move from one to the other is some melanophores to bridge the gap between the eye band and the band from the first dorsal spines—which apparently occurs in the Guyana populations and those from the Amazon. Not enough wild-caught specimens are available to me to be able to extrapolate further in the nuances of the different types of head banding. It is interesting to note at this point that *P. dumerilii* goes one step further in that there is another "short" band between the eye band and the band on the first dorsal fin spines, the eye band itself simply crossing from one eye to the other directly across the interorbital space.

Finally, there seems to be a more vertical appearance to

the Rio Orinoco individuals. Schultz considered the proportional measurements as too variable and that comparison of specimens even at "nearly equal sizes suggests that little reliance can be placed on measurements for identification purposes." The Orinoco and Rio Negro populations show a tendency to be slightly deeper bodied than the Amazon and Guyana populations in the limited material at hand. Body depth of the former ranges from 1.2-1.3 in standard length whereas that of the latter ranges from 1.3-1.5 in standard length.

Repeating the question asked before, how many *real* angelfishes are there? Answer—two, *Pterophyllum scalare* and *P. dumerilii.* But *P. scalare* is considered here to consist of two subspecies, *P. scalare scalare* from the Amazon and Guyana and *P. scalare altum* from the Orinoco and Rio Negro. These two subspecies are separable on the basis of color pattern as described above, a tendency towards higher meristic counts (at least in the dorsal and anal fin soft rays and the lateral scale rows) and perhaps a deeper body. *P. dumerilii* differs from *P. scalare* in having lower counts in the dorsal and anal fin rays and the lateral scale rows. These meristics are summarized in the accompanying table.

In addition, there are color pattern differences which can be used for distinguishing *P. scalare* and *P. dumerilii.* In *P. dumerilii* there is a conspicuous black spot located just below the dorsal fin base between the two black bars. In *P. scalare* there is a bar or the remnant of a bar in the same position, its distinctness depending a great deal upon the mood of the individual fish. As noted before, there is a separate bar between the eye band bar and the one originating at the first few dorsal fin spines. This would seem to be more similar in appearance to *P. scalare altum* from the Orinoco and Rio Negro and more distinct from the Guyana and Amazon populations. Since *P. dumerilii* has only been found in the main Amazon and Guyana regions with *P. scalare scalare,* they are more easily separated by this character from the specimens found there.

As far as known, *P. scalare scalare* has a broad range over the Amazon basin from the area of the mouth to Peru (Ucayali R., etc.) and from Guyana (Schultz also listed French Guiana in his list of specimens examined) to the Araguaia River (almost 15°S latitude near Brasilia). Dr. Axelrod was able to extend the range to the Madera River as far as Humaita.

An aquarium specimen of *Pterophyllum scalare altum.* The second head bar is weakly indicated. Photo by H.J. Richter.

SPECIES AND LOCALITIES	DORSAL FIN SPINES				DORSAL FIN RAYS														ANAL FIN SPINES			ANAL FIN RAYS													
	XI	XII	XIII	XIV	18	19	20	21	22	23	24	25	26	27	28	29	30	31	V	VI	VII	19	20	21	22	23	24	25	26	27	28	29	30	31	32
dumerilii																																			
Guyana		4			1	1	2													3			2	2											
Rio Negro-Amazon	1	8	1			3	1	2	1	1	2									10			2	2	2		1	3							
Mouth of Solimões (types of *leopoldi*)	4	20	2			7	14	5												26		1	8	11	5	1									
Mouth of Amazon		3	1							4										4							1		2		1				
Belém (holotype of *dumerilii*)		1								1										1							1								
scalare altum																																			
Upper Rio Negro		6												2	3	1				6												2	3	1	
Igarape Anapichi, Igarape Apania, Upper Rio Negro	3	21	1											1	15	6	2	1		25											1	7	10	4	2
Upper Rio Orinoco		8	1									2	3	4						9										2	3	3	1		
scalare scalare																																			
Guyana	1	20	10	2				2	7	7	10	7							2	30	1				1	5	9	4	8	4	2				
Upper Rio Araguaia		1								1										1						1									
Belém, Marajó Is.	1	8	1							3	2	1	2	1	1					10							1		2	1	3	2	1		
Pôrto do Moz		17	10						4	13	8	2							2	25						1	6	10	7	1	2				
Santarém; Óbidos; Villa Bella; Rio Cupari; Porto Negro; Monte Alegre		27	21	1				1	11	24	10	2	1							48						5	13	18	9	2	1				
Manaus; Rio Urubu; Rio Purus; Manacapurù; Coary		36	42							11	29	24	14	1					2	72	3						2	9	16	32	13	5	1		
Tefé		6	26	1						2	14	12	5							32								1	7	11	11	2			
Tonantins; Rio Jutahy; Rio Solimões; Tabatinga		9	7						1	5	5	5								16							4	4	5	2	1				
Peruvian Amazon		30	5						2	13	18	2								33	2					1	12	14	6	2					
Humaitá		2	30						9	17	6								1	31							1	10	13	6	1	1			

P. scalare altum appears to be restricted to the area from the Orinoco (at Atabapo) to the Rio Negro at least as far as Igarape Anapichi and Igarape Apania. The Orinoco and Rio Negro may have some connection through the Casiquiare River (where *P. s. altum* has also been found).

P. dumerilii seems to be restricted to the Amazon River from its mouth to Tonantins on the Solimoes, as well as occurring in Guyana. Its distribution seems to follow that of *P. scalare scalare,* although it is not nearly as widespread or common. Perhaps as the species becomes better known its distributional pattern will become clearer.

Counts recorded for *Pterophyllum* species at various localities in the Amazon basin and adjacent regions. Data from Schultz, 1967 and new material.

SPECIES AND LOCALITIES	SCALES																					
	26	27	28	29	30	31	32	33	34	35	36	37	38	39	40	41	42	43	44	45	46	47
dumerilii																						
Guyana			1	2																		
Rio Negro-Amazon	1	2	2		3	1		1														
Mouth of Solimöes (types of *leopoldi*)	1	3	9	8	4	1																
Mouth of Amazon					1	3																
Belém (holotype of *dumerilii*)					1																	
scalare altum																						
Upper Rio Negro											3	1			1	2	2			1		
Igarape Anapichi, Igarape Apania, Upper Rio Negro															5	4	2	2	2	4	2	2
Upper Rio Orinoco									2	1	4	1	3		1	1	1	2				
scalare scalare																						
Guyana			1	3	3	3	4	2	3	4	2	1	2	2	2							
Upper Rio Araguaia									1													
Belém, Marajó Is.						3		2						1		1	2		1			
Pôrto do Moz				1	1	3	4	7	4	4	2	1										
Santarém; Óbidos; Villa Bella; Rio Cupari; Porto Negro; Monte Alegre				1	5	4	9	11	10	7	1	1	2									
Manaus; Rio Urubu; Rio Purus; Manacapurù; Coary						3	4	6	10	18	14	13	7	1		1	1					
Tefé						1	1	4	4	6	6	4	3	2	1							
Tonantins; Rio Jutahy; Rio Solimöes; Tabatinga					1	2	5	2	1		3		2									
Peruvian Amazon					2	8	4	7	6	3	4	1										
Humaitá					1		4	1	2	6		2										

A pair of blacklace veiltail angelfish. Crossing these two will produce a mixture of forms. Photo by Dr. Herbert R. Axelrod. *Right:* One of the first photos of the true all black angelfish. This strain eluded breeders for a long time but became established by 1955. Photo by Gene Wolfsheimer.

Varieties and Genetics

By Dr. Warren E. Burgess

In the early 1900's (the date actually given is 1911) the first angelfish, probably specimens of *Pterophyllum scalare,* were imported into Europe. They became an immediate hit with aquarists although attempts at spawning them were more often than not doomed to failure. This difficulty of spawning wild-caught angelfishes, especially from the areas outside of the mainstream of the Amazon River, persists even to this day. But dedicated aquarists overcame the difficulties and succeeded in eventually producing angelfishes domestically in quantity. In time mutations and sports appeared that were seized upon by breeders to produce the many varieties that can be seen today.

Among the most diligently pursued, and perhaps the most legendary aquarium fish of its time, was the all-black angelfish. Rumor after rumor surfaced that a pure black angel was near at hand, but there never seemed to be actual fish to back them up. About 1953 it was reported that some dark or partially black angels appeared "spontaneously" in Europe. By 1955 or so several claims were made that true black angelfish were being produced in numbers. Whether these came from the European stock or developed independently in this country (or both, which seems most likely) cannot be determined, but the aquarium literature soon broke the story complete with photographs—the all-black angelfish had arrived! Although not all these strains were true-breeding, some of them were and, in spite of the delicate and difficult-to-breed nature of these black angelfish, their numbers increased in leaps and bounds.

The all-black angelfish are, as the name implies, a solid black color. They are true-breeding; a cross between two solid black fish will produce only solid blacks. Some strains were called all-black but in truth were not for they did not have the genuine black color and when crossed even produced some silver angels.

The blacklace angelfish looks similar to the normal silver angelfish but with a general darkening of the silver areas, though not so much as to obscure the striped pattern. The lace effect is produced by the darkening pattern in the fins. It is a very attractive fish and may have been the forerunner to the all-black strain. A gene for darkness probably appeared as a mutation and was inbred until the fish became solid black. If this gene for black color is called "B" and the corresponding gene for the non-black or normal color is called "b," then the blacklace angelfish has a complement recorded as Bb and the all-black strain as BB. The all-blacks then get a 'double dose' of the black character. It can be seen that when an all-black (BB) is crossed with a normal silver angel (bb) only blacklace young (Bb) are produced.

When two blacklace parents are crossed (Bb X Bb) you get a mixture of all-black (BB), blacklace (Bb) and silver (bb) in the ratio of 25%, 50% and 25% respectively. This is of course theoretical. In actuality the numbers will vary somewhat. If the ratios are observed when the youngsters are a few months old it will be seen that the survival rates differ considerably. There will be a greater percentage of normal angels surviving than blacks, which are rather delicate. The blacklace survival is somewhere in between. If more blacks are to survive they must be separated from the others and given individual treatment for they cannot compete for food with the more vigorous silvers.

A second major strain was started in Germany about 1956. In a batch of silver angels there appeared a fish with unusually long fins. With careful cross breeding, similar to what was done with the all-black angelfish, the long fins were not only established but greatly lengthened. The veiltail was born! The veiltail angelfish has a pattern similar to the normal silver angelfish but the dorsal, anal and caudal fins have become elongated. The genetics of this strain are similar to that of the black angels. If the veiltail character is considered as V and the non-veiltail as v, a veiltail with long fins would be Vv. However, if there is a double dose of veiltail genes, VV, the fins are greatly elongate. A cross between two mixed (heterozygous) veiltails (Vv X Vv) would yield, theoretically, 25% silver (vv), 50% veiltail (Vv) and 25% super veiltail (VV).

What would happen then if one were to cross a blacklace angel with a veiltail? This was tried and resulted in blacklace veiltail, combining features of both. Crossing blacklace veiltail with blacklace veiltail (BbVv X BbVv) gives quite a mixture. Out of every 16 individuals the theoretical proportion would be as follows: 1 silver, 1 black, 2 blacklace, 3 veiltails, 3 black veiltails and 6 blacklace veiltails. One of these veiltails, one black veiltail and two of the blacklace veiltails are of the VV type, the others Vv. Unlike the pure black angels, the veiltails seem to be relatively easy to breed.

Also in the early 1950's a half-black angelfish was developed. This angel, as the name implies, was partially black. The area posterior to a line drawn through the middle of the dorsal and anal fins was black, anterior to this it was normally patterned. They eventually disappeared but reappeared in the late 1960's. At neither time did they become very popular and at present they are quite scarce.

The next major strain to be developed first appeared in 1963 as a mutant individual (along with an albino which will be discussed later) in a batch of normal angels. It was not until the late 1960's that the marble angel first made its debut in numbers. Again it started as a mutant or sport in a batch of normal silver angels. It was separated from the silver angels and placed with some blacklace angels, upon maturity, to spawn. The progeny, however, were all silver although the bar pattern seemed quite dark. Several males were backcrossed to their mother (the mutant) until eventually three more marble angels appeared. At this point there were male and female marble angels which were inbred to produce a purer strain.

The marble angelfish has the ordinary silver background of the silver angels but instead of the black bars it has large blotches and/or streaks of black creating a marbleized pattern. The dorsal, anal and caudal fins have streaks of black through them producing a very pleasing and sometimes dramatically beautiful effect. In many marble angels the head region has a decided yellow color. The pattern of each fish is different and any aquarist can pick and choose those that most please him. The genetics of the marble angelfish follows the same pattern as that of the black angelfish and veiltails. The single marble (Mm) when compared to the double marble (MM) does not appear that different although it has been reported that there are light forms and dark forms of marble angelfish, the dark form being the one that is homozygous (MM) rather than heterozygous (Mm) for the character.

The next step of course would be to try to mix the marble angel with the above black and veiltail strains. This was accomplished and a truly beautiful marble veiltail angel was developed as well as a blacklace marble. This latter fish appears similar to the dark marble form but has some of the blacklace pattern as well.

The first golden angelfish was discovered quite by accident. A small individual was discovered in a batch of regular angels. It was first assumed to be a runt, the type of individuals good breeders usually cull out of their flocks. But this one was put aside and generally ignored. As it grew the pattern became more blotchy, another cause for it to be discarded, but it was still saved. Finally the black disappeared and the fish turned from a dull gray to a bright yellow. It was then recognized as something special, and crossbreeding procedures finally resulted in more of them. Unfortunately it took six to nine months for the black pigment to eventually disappear, but concentrated breeding efforts reduced this to three months. At that time, around 1969, they were ready for marketing. Soon after (in the early 1970's) a second golden strain was developed. Can you imagine how many "runts" and blotchy angels were culled that might have become golden angels? This was a true ugly duckling that turned into a beautiful swan.

Two interesting sidelights occurred in connection with the early golden angelfish. In about 10% of the individuals the black pigment disappeared from the eyes as well as the body, creating, in effect, what appeared like an albino. It was not a true albino since there was originally black pigment. Only one true albino, born without black pigmentation and with pink eyes, was found and it occurred along with the mutant that started the marble angelfish strain. Unfortunately the original albino was blind and no further albinos were able to be produced from that individual. The

1 2

3

(1) A natural wild type *Pterophyllum scalare.* One of the characters is the presence of reddish spots on the back. (2) One of the wild-caught specimens of *Pterophyllum dumerilii* with dark spot and two short head bands. (3) *Pterophyllum scalare altum* from the Orinoco. Note the long dorsal and anal fins and red spots. Photos by Dr. Herbert R. Axelrod.

second interesting thing about the golden angel was that when it was frightened the dark bars appeared, only to fade out again when the fish calmed down. These were from the second strain and appeared to develop the golden color early in life (as soon as the youngsters took on their angelfish shape) but did not become an intensely yellow as the early strain. In addition, none of the eyes lost their black pigmentation. This goes to show how much genetic variability there is even within a so-called strain.

It was not long before the golden and veiltail angels were crossed to produce the golden veiltail. The genetics, however, have still not been worked out as yet and the two golden strains, which seem to have different genetic make ups, may eventually lead to something even better.

As if the above varieties were not enough, an additional strain was developed in which the black bars disappeared. This was dubbed the ghost angelfish or white ghost. This was carried a step further, wherein not only the black bars disappeared but the general coloration of the fish became more translucent. In the gill area the pigmentation became so reduced that the red color of the gills themselves was visible through the opercula. The pale fish with the reddish "cheeks" was named the blushing or bleeding heart angelfish. The bleeding heart appears to be the result of a double dose of the blushing gene, a single dose resulting in the white ghost. In other words, if the blushing angel and a silver angel were crossed you would get only white angelfish. When these progeny are crossed the result is a mixture of blushing, white and silver. If two blushing angelfish were crossed you would get only blushing just as when you cross two all-black angelfish you get only all-black angelfish.

Needless to say, the blushing angels were crossed with all the other varieties producing blushing blacklace angels, blushing veiltails, blushing marble angels and half-black blushing angelfish.

Fairly recently a strain has been developed in which there are three major black bars crossing the body instead of two (with a hint of the third). Appropriately enough this has been called the zebra angelfish and appears to have been developed from the blacklace variety.

With many aquarists breeding angelfish there are bound to be sports or mutants that show up from time to time. In one case a few individuals of a black and gold or a black, silver and gold form appeared but the strains were never set and this type has not appeared in any numbers. But the angelfish breeders are still enthusiastic about new strains and become almost glassy-eyed when they start to dream about the possibility of the blue angelfish or the red angelfish. (A green angelfish was reported but it turned out to be the result of feeding hormones rather than a true strain although if the green color can be produced artificially maybe . . .)

One problem about these different varieties or strains—most of them are weaker than the original silver angelfish and are much more difficult to breed. Silver angelfish are the strongest and the marble next. The blacklace is weaker than the marble and the black is weaker than the blacklace. The blushing angel is weaker yet than the black, and perhaps the most delicate of all is the blushing veiltail.

A pair of golden veiltail angelfish in the process of spawning. Photo by Peter Wong. *Right:* A golden angel (black pigments fading out) spawning with a blushing angel (red gill area) on a broad leaf. Photos by H.J. Richter.

An Atypical Singapore Fish Operation

By Dr. Herbert R. Axelrod

In August, 1974, I celebrated my 25th visit to Singapore by visiting some of my old friends. As usual, I found Singapore fish dealers among the world's most active. In this small city (which is also a state and country) they ship out more than $6,000,000 worth of guppies per year!! Fish are their most economically important replenishable commodity, and the government encourages the people to raise fish.

The dealers are, among themselves, very competitive. They have very active tropical fish societies and are highly competitive in the world fish market. I can safely say that Singapore-raised fishes are excellent in terms of price, quality and health . . . and Singapore exporters (with certain few exceptions) are good businessmen.

I visited two friends, James Poh Kui, 36E, Jervois Road, Singapore 10, and my old and trusted friends of the firm of Straits Aquarium, 20 Soon Hock Road, Singapore 20. I give their addresses in case you want to contact them (it will save me from having to answer hundreds of inquiries).

About ten years ago I sent Straits some of the beautiful angelfish which were raised by Karl Naja, the famous Milwaukee fish breeder. They were from the "albino" strain which spent the first six to eight months of their lives being normally colored. When I sent them to Wilson Yeo Eng Nam, the Director of The Straits Aquarium, I asked him to please breed the angelfish and keep track of his breeding results . . . "AND DO NOT SELL ANY FISH FOR ONE YEAR!!!" Imagine his surprise when after half a year or so his normally-colored angelfish started to turn into beautiful reds, whites and blotched beauties. They even lost color in their eyes. Wilson was quite excited about this variety, and he soon became the world's largest breeder of them.

When I visited Wilson on this trip, I took a pair to Germany to show them to a German wholesaler, Heiko Bleher. Bleher is the world's largest dealer in rare South American fishes. He specializes in different species of discus. Heiko thought it would be impractical to bring them into Germany because the people wouldn't have the patience for fish to change colors. So I took them with me to Leipzig, East Germany, and presented them to the fish photographer Hans-Joachim Richter, the pride of the Deutsche Demokratische Republik (DDR). Unfortunately I didn't have a chance to tell Richter the whole story about these fish, as I had to leave immediately for Africa, but when I returned to Leipzig exactly ten days later, Richter had spawned the fish and made a beautiful series of color photographs of the spawning. Richter is not only a great photographer but also an outstanding fish breeder. He has probably spawned more species of fishes than any other non-commercial person. He only breeds fishes for the purpose of gathering information and photographs.

Anyway, I thought it would be a nice joke if I didn't tell Richter about the angelfish having normal babies! As time went on and the babies grew, Richter became quite curious. Why were they not like their parents? Of course I didn't say anything at all, and during my frequent visits (every few months) to Leipzig, I just noticed his tanks becoming filled with thousands of normal baby angelfish. Of course, every time the fishes spawned, Richter would photograph them, and since the color changes in the adult fish were so slow, Richter hardly noticed that the fish which were originally blotched had progressively lost more and more of their color! Richter is too intelligent a fish breeder to be fooled for long. Finally he said: "Herbert, you wise guy, these are the famous Karl Naja angelfish from Milwaukee. Here I have thousands of babies and not a single one has changed colors!" That was six months ago. I just got another batch of spawning photos from Richter with a note . . . "The Naja angelfish are changing colors!"

Wilson specializes in many other fishes besides angelfish. He also bred the first strain of big-bellied molly which must now be given a common name. Wilson spent years working on the strain and producing them in black and green, both with sailfins and lyretails. He calls them "balloon mollies." Anyway, for better or for worse, this is now the balloon molly from Singapore, and the whole aquarium world owes Straits Aquarium a vote of thanks. Straits, by the way, said he was inspired by the various Chinese goldfish which had the same form, so he carefully inbred a sport which appeared as a runt among his annual production of millions of mollies to produce the balloon molly. Of course Richter was appalled at the sight of the fish and he photographed them for me with great displeasure, saying they were cripples and not worthy of being kept in aquariums of civilized people. What I like about them is that they are so hardy. They are small and develop lovely high fins . . . and they

The golden angel loses its black pigments as it grows. Here are two photos showing the same specimen (note the yellow spot in caudal fin) with the remainder of its black bands (opposite page) and after they have completely gone (above). The dark blotch in the dorsal fin will eventually disappear also. Photos by H. J. Richter.

don't get the shimmies which eventually kill most mollies raised in Florida. Try'em, you might like 'em!

James Poh Kui took me to one of his contract fish farmers, a chap named Ng Swee Yong, 90F Sungei Tengah Road, Singapore 24. Mr. Ng (the Chinese put their family name first; thus my name in Chinese would read Axelrod Herbert) was the first one in Singapore . . . and probably the world . . . to breed albino chocolate mollies, and he decorated them with sailfins and lyretails.

An interesting part of Ng's operation was his discus hatchery. Some 20 years ago I first reported on the use of kerosine lamps to keep discus tanks over 85° in order to keep the discus happy and in spawning condition. Ng took note of this and went out to buy some kerosine lamps. He has been successful in discus-raising ever since, and he now produces 20,000 young discus for sale every year. When the babies are a month old, they are put outdoors; of course they are kept with their parents for the first month so they can feed on the slime produced on the parents' bodies.

Ng and the rest of the fish farmers in Singapore are lucky. They just set their tanks outdoors and don't worry about heat or storms. The temperature might drop down to 76° at night, but that's doubtful. All it takes in Singapore to start a fish farm is some land, tanks and wood to make pools. The pools are shaded with corrugated galvanized sheeting, and the dirt pools are fed with stale rice (if there is such a thing), lettuce leaves, etc., to support a rich growth of *Daphnia*. The fishes are fed *Daphnia* and Wardley's flake foods.

Ng believes in keeping his discus and their babies in almost complete darkness since, he says, "That's the way the water looks in the Rio Negro of Brazil where they come from." (He's right about the black water . . . you can't see much in 10 feet of black Amazonian water!) He feeds the breeders *Daphnia, Tubifex* and brine shrimp.

Mr. Ng sells only to the local market (he doesn't export)

and has been a fish breeder for 17 years. His 2-acre farm produces goldfish, swordtails, platies, barbs, angelfish, gouramis and discus. He has three helpers and traps rainwater in a large pool to pump into his tanks for slow changes of water.

After my tour, Wilson took me back home and I had a 12-course home-cooked Chinese dinner that was certainly the finest I ever had in my life . . . and all 13 members of the family watched me gorge myself! If you ever get to Singapore, you won't find anyone nicer and more hospitable than the Chinese fish people . . . and the folks at The Straits Aquarium are among the finest.

From left to right are Wilson Lim An Loo, Ng Swee Yong, and James Poh Kui standing next to one of the fish pools. Photo by Dr. Herbert R. Axelrod.

A blushing angel female depositing eggs. Photo by H.J. Richter. *Below:* The potential spawning site must first be thoroughly cleaned by the prospective parents. Photo by H.J. Richter.

Breeding and Raising Angelfishes

By Dr. Warren E. Burgess

Angelfishes are among the most popular of freshwater aquarium fishes, along with such perennial favorites as the guppy and neon tetra. As such they are in great demand almost all of the time. The supplies are usually adequate, however, since they are also relatively easy to breed and produce a fairly substantial number of eggs and fry. But there are problems involved, and any potential angelfish breeder must keep in mind certain bits of information if he is to maintain any measure of success.

First of all, when angelfishes are said to be hardy, easy to breed and easy to raise, it must be understood that these characteristics are meant to pertain to the silver angelfish—the normal, everyday, domestic strain silver angelfish. When we talk about the more fancy varieties and wild-caught angelfishes, that is something else entirely. From their first importation, wild-caught angelfishes were notoriously difficult to breed. Even to this day, with all the experience gained from years of breeding the domestic strains, the imported stock still refuse to cooperate. Importations of the Orinoco angelfish (*P. altum* of aquarists) as recently as 1975 gave angelfish breeders another chance at this elusive fish, but so far there have been no glowing reports of successes. Keeping them alive was even considered a difficult task since they did not seem to respond to the same treatment given to the domestic varieties. The domestic strains of today are far removed from the first specimens imported way back in 1911, and it seems that in the elapsed period of time the water conditions under which they are now kept are very different from those in which they started and from those in their natural habitat. Although some books will tell you that the angelfishes can be kept under a wide variety of water conditions, many of the breeders recommend a pH of 6.8-7.2 (or more) and a hardness of 6-9 DH (100-150ppm) for the breeding tank. Just recently the water was analyzed at the collecting site of the Orinoco angelfish and found to be quite different from that just recorded. The pH was more acid, with a range of from 5.8-6.2, and the water was much softer, with a hardness measurement of 1 DH. Perhaps this information will be instrumental in aiding the prospective breeder of wild-caught Orinoco angelfish in his endeavors.

To obtain any measure of success in breeding angelfish (or any fish for that matter), one must start with good stock. After all, you cannot expect to produce a perfect angelfish from parents that are less than perfect themselves. So a little extra care in selecting the breeders will go a long way toward beautifully developed, well-patterned progeny. Look for perfect fins, that is, those which are not underdeveloped, are well proportioned and in which the rays are all straight. Make sure the color pattern is good and strong (remembering of course that the bars of the angelfish will turn dark when it is frightened) and that the fish is of a proper size for its age. It may be a great feeling to be able to take a poor forlorn little critter from its larger and more domineering tankmates and grow it up to be more beautiful than any of them, but all too many times the little ugly duckling grows up to be a medium sized ugly duckling and stays that way. For breeding purposes go for the perfect specimens. Select those with overall better vitality than those that are more listless.

How many angelfish should one start with? The minimum of course is two, one male and one female, providing they are a compatible pair. It is difficult enough to choose a pair, what with the differences between the sexes all but nonexistent, without having to worry about whether they will get along together or not. For this reason it is best to leave the selection of individual fish to experts. If your dealer is one of these experts you are in luck, especially if he will back up his choice with a guarantee that if the fish are not what he says they are, they (or one of them anyway) can be exchanged for the proper sex. A second method of getting a compatible breeding pair, and one which is almost 100% certain, is to buy a pair that has already bred. You can be sure that they are male and female if they have produced viable eggs and fry, and you can be sure that they are a compatible pair if they have already spawned, but you cannot be sure that they will repeat their performance for you. Something in your water, your tank, your food or even your actions may influence the pair to call it quits. That is the risk you have to take. Considering the cost of true mated pairs, this might be a risk you are not willing to take.

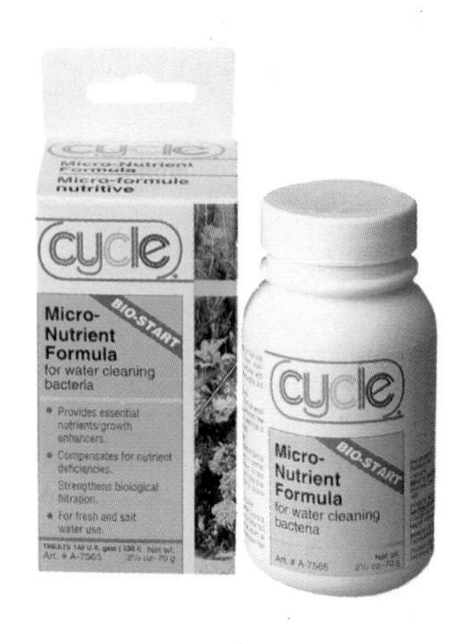

Bacteria that live within a biological filtration system have to be provided with nutrients in order to become established in an aquarium, and products that provide those nutrients are available at pet shops and tropical fish specialty stores. Photo courtesy of Hagen.

Wet/dry filtration systems, which provide a very large surface area on which the beneficial bacteria that form the basis of a biological filtration system live, are available in sizes to fit both large and relatively small tanks. Photo courtesy of Hagen.

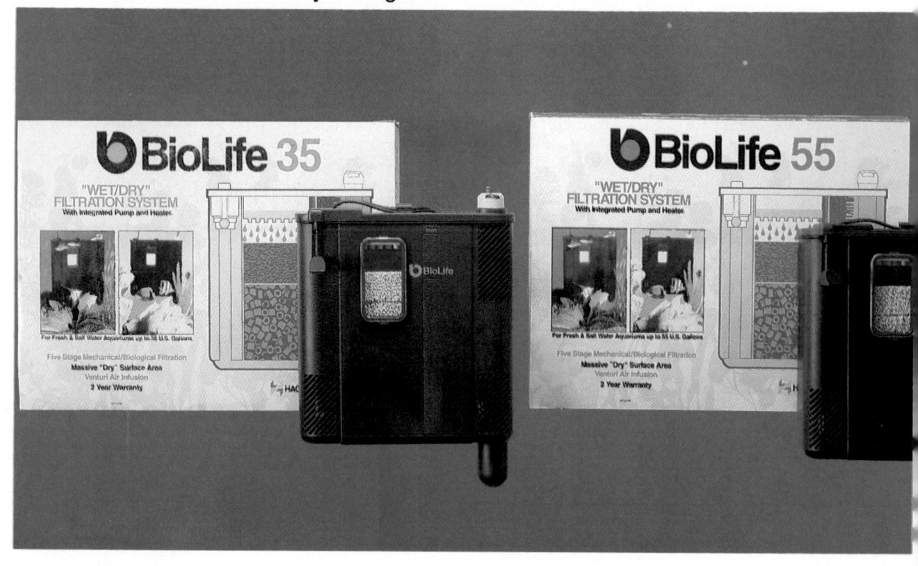

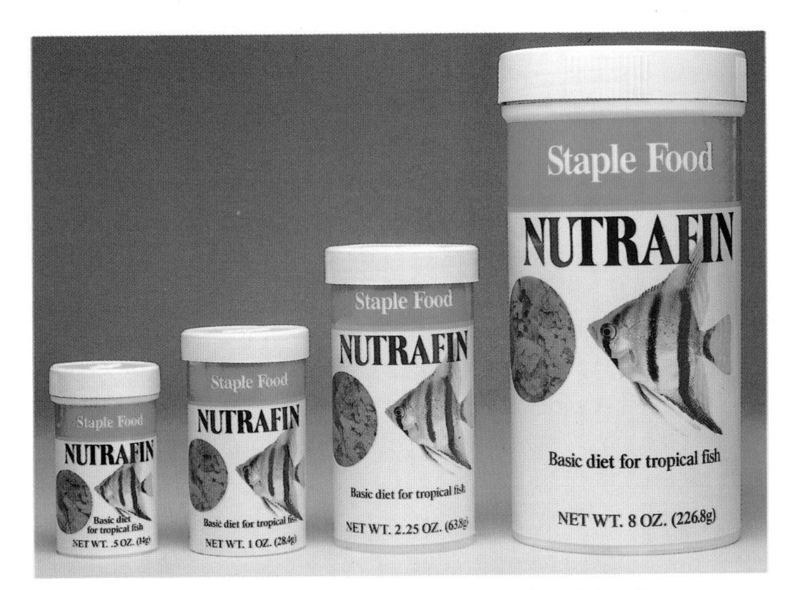

Above: There are many different foods for aquarium fishes in general and angelfishes in particular, and they come in different forms as well. Foods in the form of flakes, for example, are among the most popular. Photo courtesy of Hagen.

Below: A wide range of disease preventives and remedies designed to cure or ward off the most common maladies of angelfishes and other tropicals is available at pet shops. Photo courtesy of Jungle Laboratories.

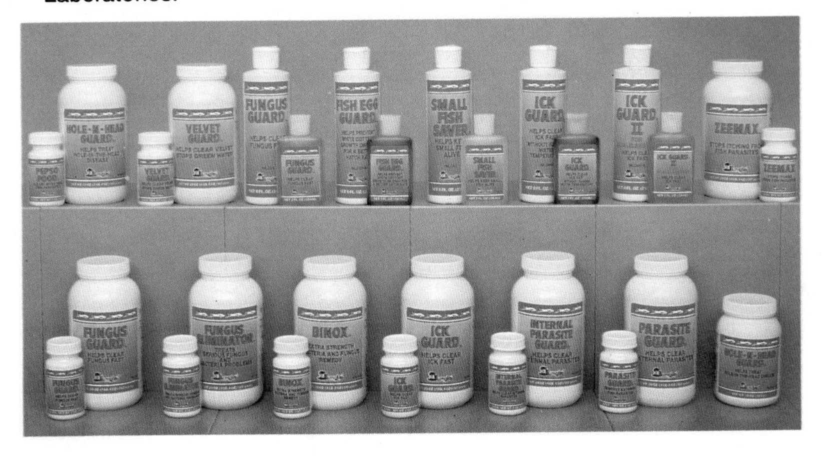

For those who have the time and the room, the best method seems to be to obtain up to a dozen small individuals and raise them in a fairly large tank—at least a 50-gallon tank—with the expectation that when they reach adulthood they will pair up by themselves. More than one pair will probably be obtained this way, and you can have more than one breeding tank going at a time. Of course the minimum number statistically in which you will be almost certain to have at least one male and one female, provided the fish were selected randomly, is six. When you increase the number from six you increase your chances of getting more than one pair.

Since angelfish are available in many different sizes (and at many different prices), you can select the size that most suits your needs. If you are impatient and can afford larger fishes, by all means buy the larger ones. The larger they are the better you can tell whether or not they are in good shape. Be careful of the real bargain fish. The low price might be there for a good reason. Many times people have happily returned home with bags full of fishes which they got at bargain prices only to find out a short time later that it was money thrown away for they all died. Or after several months the small bargain fishes are still small and not so much of a bargain anymore. But that is not to say that really good stock cannot be picked up at bargain prices. Just be warned that you should be careful in your purchases.

Breeding tanks are usually kept separate from the tanks that house the group of angels. The community tank can be set up with the usual decorations (rocks, gravel, plants) and even include other compatible species as well. The angels can be watched for signs of pairing, after which they are moved to a specially set up breeding tank. The breeding tank can be smaller than 50 gallons athough not too small. Although angels have been successfully spawned in ten-gallon aquaria, it is strongly recommended that one twice that size or larger be used. The larger tank will be easier to maintain and the breeding pair will be more at ease in the more spaceous quarters. The tank can be relatively bare except for some Amazon swordplants or other broad-leaved forms which will afford the fish some protection as well as a place upon which to lay the eggs. A piece of flat slate placed at about a 45° angle in the tank will provide yet another surface for them and will also give them a choice of substrates. Some angelfish will ignore both plant and slate and wind up spawning on the glass of the aquarium. Aeration and filtration systems can be used for the breeding tank, keeping in mind the delicate nature of the eggs and fry.

The spawning tank can be set up at the first signs of pairing in the community tank. This will first be observed as an increase in the general activity of the angelfish. There will be sparring between the fish, some mock fights and then when things get really serious, actual mouth or jaw wrestling. Those individuals that actually pair up usually stay together and will often claim a section of the tank as their own, making sure none of the other angels are allowed to trespass. At this point they can be removed to the breeding tank. The water in this tank should be approximately equivalent to the community tank so that there will be no complications when they are moved. The pH should be around 7.2 and the hardness 6-9 DH (100-150ppm). The temperature, if maintained at about 78° in the community tank, can be edged up slowly in the breeding tank to about 80°F. It is then up to the angelfish. Be sure to feed them a goodly supply of the most nutritious foods on the market.

With patience and understanding, it will not be too long before your angelfish spawn. About two days before actual egg-laying the female's breeding tube descends. This can be seen as a large blunt object protruding from the vent area. The male's breeding tube is smaller and more pointed and descends on the actual day that spawning will take place. The appearance of the breeding tubes may not be a sure

1

A spawning sequence involving a pair of marble angelfish. (1) The usual cleaning of the spawning site. (2) The deposition and fertilization of the eggs. (3) A close-up of the eggs. The eggs are attached to the substrate (leaf, slate, glass, etc.) by sticky filaments and are not easy to dislodge. Photos by H.J. Richter.

2 3

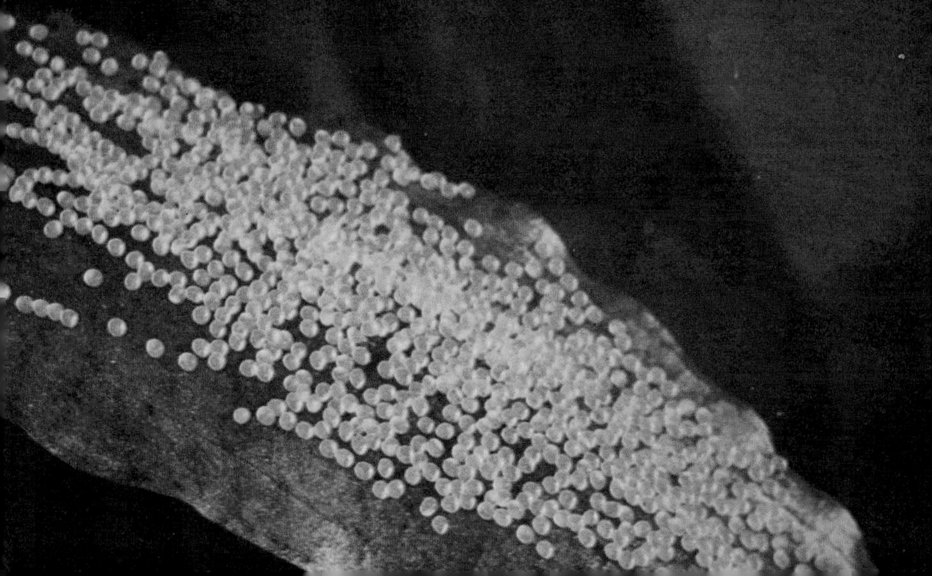

sign of impending spawning, but it is certainly a good sign. The potential parents at this time will also begin to actively clean a section of the slate or one of the broad leaves of the Amazon swordplant. Again, this is a good sign but by no means guarantees that actual egg-laying will take place. Something might disturb or distract the pair and the spawning is forgotten for the time being. Now things begin to get more delicate and the presence of the aquarist may actually be one of the distractions that affect the spawning. It may be better for the first spawning at least to simply discover the eggs after spawning rather than to sit and wait expectantly for the pair to get on with their spawning. If the aquarist is quiet and the pair not too disturbed by his presence, the female then passes over the cleaned portion of the leaf or of the slate a few times with her genital papilla almost or just touching it. The eggs are eventually deposited in this manner in strings of a dozen or so with the male following behind fertilizing them. After each string is laid the female will circle around and get into position for placing the next string, usually in close proximity to the last. The male follows her, and as the new eggs are deposited he fertilizes them. This continues until as many as 600 eggs are laid. Normal spawns are more in the order of 300-400 but may be as few as 100 in females that are small, young or not in the best of health.

From this point on every minute that the parents are left with the eggs means that the aquarist is risking having them devoured by one or both of the parents. If they are good parents, however, they take far better care of the eggs than the aquarist can manage. They will fan them with their fins, creating currents of water that flow over them carrying off the carbon dioxide that is released in respiration and providing a more abundant supply of necessary oxygen, defend them from all intruders both real and imaginary and remove any of them that are attacked by fungus. Unfortunately, not all angelfish are such good parents and it takes only one to finish off the entire spawn. This attacking of the eggs (and fry after they have hatched) can occur at any time, even after the parents have carefully tended the eggs for awhile!

If the eggs are left alone they hatch in about two days and the fry can be seen hanging from the leaf or slate by a thread. Within this time one or both of the parents may select another spot to clean and soon after hatching move the fry to this new, clean spot. The old site is abandoned, perhaps because of the decaying egg shells or because in nature to remain in the same spot for too long a time might invite outside predators. Moving the fry from place to place probably gives the parents a chance to place them in a more defensible position. At the end of about five days the fry become free-swimming and start to look for food.

For those of faint heart, the eggs can be removed from their parents and hatched by artificial means. This simply means lifting out the piece of slate or detaching the leaf upon which they were laid. This can be placed in a small aquarium or jar that has been cleaned very thoroughly and filled with clean water. There have been many discussions as to whether or not to use clean water straight from the tap or aged water from the breeding tank. Proponents of old water usage say that the eggs should not be subjected to the drastic changes that fresh tap water would expose them to, whereas those who favor fresh water usage say that the eggs should not be placed in bacteria - or fungus-laden water and that the chlorine in the tap water will help destroy those organisms that are carried in with the eggs. For those who want to compromise, they can simply take fresh tap water and age it as well as bring the chemical composition as close to that of the breeding tank water as possible. For safety a little fungicide can be added. The eggs need the circulation of water that the fanning of the parents provides and a good substitute is a well-placed airstone. The airstone should be placed close enough to the eggs so that there will be ade-

One of the weaker strains of angelfish, the blushing veiltail. This strain is produced by crossing a blushing angel with a silver veiltail. Photo by Ray Juschkus.

A newer strain with extra body stripes called the zebra angelfish. Photo by H.J. Richter.

quate circulation but far enough so that no damage will befall the eggs or newly hatched fry. Any eggs that do fungus must be removed by hand using a sterilized pair of tweezers.

The eggs hatch in the same time as they would if the parents were present and become free-swimming in the same length of time—about five days.

For the first couple of weeks the angelfish fry can be fed on newly hatched brine shrimp. Those who recommend infusoria as the first food are becoming fewer and fewer. After about two weeks supplemental foods can be added and the youngsters are on their way. In about three weeks they begin to look a bit like their parents, and in 2½ months they have a body size of about a quarter.

Make sure that the young are adequately fed (and the parents also if they have been allowed to remain with their progeny) and that the tank is kept as clean as possible in spite of the feedings. A small siphon is an excellent tool for this purpose, but make sure that the fry are not inadvertently sucked in by the siphon along with the unwanted material. At the same time partial water changes can be made, starting slowly with 10% to 20% when the fry become free-swimming and increasing the amount up to nearly 50% by the time they are two months old.

When the parents are left with the fry they can be seen to pick individual fry from their position on the slate or leaf from time to time and mouth them, spitting them out again into the mass of wriggling fry. This is also done in conjunction with their moving from one spot to another in the tank. After they become free-swimming, the youngsters spread out through the tank searching for food, with the parents seeming to tolerate this but all the time keeping a wary eye open for anything amiss. At feeding time the parents should be given their own food as well, and it appears that they can easily distinguish between the food they are supposed to eat and their own progeny. At night the fry are kept in a close school where the parents can more easily watch over them. Any youngster who dares to venture too far from this group is immediately returned by one of the parents. Eventually the young grow too large for this sort of thing and spread out through the tank to stay and fend for themselves.

1

2

(1) When spawning is completed one or both parents remain close to the eggs fanning them with their fins. (2) If any of the eggs fungus the attending parent will remove them from the spawning site (a piece of slate was used here by this silver veiltail).

FRESHWATER
ANGELFISHES
KW-048